GREENHOUSE GARDENING
for Beginners

Darren Sutton

GREENHOUSE GARDENING FOR BEGINNERS

The content contained within this book may not be reproduced, duplicated or transmitted without direct written permission from the author or the publisher.

Under no circumstances will any blame or legal responsibility be held against the publisher, or author, for any damages, reparation, or monetary loss due to the information contained within this book. Either directly or indirectly.

Legal Notice:

This book is copyright protected. This book is only for personal use. You cannot amend, distribute, sell, use, quote or paraphrase any part, or the content within this book, without the consent of the author or publisher.

Disclaimer Notice:

Please note the information contained within this document is for educational and entertainment purposes only. All effort has been executed to present accurate, up to date, and reliable, complete information. No warranties of any kind are declared or implied. Readers acknowledge that the author is not engaging in the rendering of legal, financial, medical or professional advice. The content within this book has been derived from various sources. Please consult a licensed professional before attempting any techniques outlined in this book.

By reading this document, the reader agrees that under no circumstances is the author responsible for any losses, direct or indirect, which are incurred as a result of the use of information contained within this document, including, but not limited to, — errors, omissions, or inaccuracies.

Copyright @ 2023 by Darren Sutton

GREENHOUSE GARDENING FOR BEGINNERS

CONTENT

5   Introduction

CHAPTER 1
GREENHOUSE BASICS
7   1.1 Choose The Right Greenhouse
13   1.2 Kinds of Greenhouses
16   1.3 Create Greenhouse Environment
21   1.4 Basic Greenhouse Accessories
25   1.5 Seed Starting

CHAPTER 2
GREENHOUSE EQUIPMENT
33   2.1 Greenhouse Drainage And Irrigation Equipment
26   2.2 Furniture To Store Your Plants And Greenhouse Equipment

CHAPTER 3
GREENHOUSE PLANTS
39   3.1 Beginners' Guide to Growing Easy Greenhouse Plants
60   3.2 Growing Vegetable Herbs, And Fruit
64   3.3 The Best Food To Grow In A Greenhouse
68   3.4 Growing Without Soil
74   3.5 Selecting The Right Plants
78   3.6 Planting In A Warm And Cold Weather
88   3.7 Scheduling plants for the year-round growing

CHAPTER 4
MAINTAINING THE GREENHOUSE
95   4.1 Maintenance
99   4.2 High Tunnels, Low Tunnels, Coldframes, Hoop Houses, and Polytunnels

CHAPTER 5
MAKING A PROFIT
103   5.1 Why Greenhouse Business?
104   5.2 Make Money Growing Vegetables in Greenhouses
105   5.3 Growing Flowers in a Greenhouse for Profit
109   5.4 Your Responsibilities

111   Conclusion

GREENHOUSE GARDENING FOR BEGINNERS

GREENHOUSE GARDENING FOR BEGINNERS

Introduction

A greenhouse is nothing more than a structure used to cultivate plants. These structures might be quite small or rather large. The concept of greenhouses dates back to Roman times when Emperor Tiberius compelled his gardeners to utilize a system similar to modern greenhouses.

The first modern greenhouses date back to 13th-century Italy. Greenhouses were initially more widespread on rich estates but gradually extended to universities. The nineteenth-century saw some of the largest greenhouses ever built, while the twentieth century saw the widespread use of the geodesic dome in greenhouses.

The purpose of a greenhouse is to protect crops from extreme cold or heat and hazardous pests. A greenhouse enables the year-round production of specific crops, with vegetables, tobacco plants, fruits, and flowers being the most often grown crops in a greenhouse. Due to concerns about ensuring a healthy food supply. For example, Almeria, Spain, is home to one of the largest greenhouses in the world, covering 50,000 acres.

The primary purpose of a greenhouse garden is to lengthen the growing season of treasured crops and plants. Horticulture enthusiasts should also be enthused about greenhouses since they allow for the year-round cultivation of plants and flowers that can subsequently be taken into the house. A greenhouse garden can be constructed inexpensively or ex-

GREENHOUSE GARDENING FOR BEGINNERS

travagantly, using plastic or glass, and can be appealing or just utilitarian in appearance. After selecting an ideal place for your greenhouse garden, you can construct one yourself by obtaining a greenhouse kit from one of several renowned manufacturers. These do-it-yourself projects can be as intricate or simple as desired, huge or small.

Chapter 1
Greenhouse Basics

1.1 Choose The Right Greenhouse

There are several alternatives available when it comes to acquiring a greenhouse. If you're new to greenhouse gardening, you might want to start with something simple and inexpensive. Maybe you already have a small greenhouse and are looking to expand. You should use caution while purchasing a greenhouse, regardless of your motive for doing so.

1. Look for a greenhouse with features that will help you extend your growing season.

You should be able to grow all year in a well-designed greenhouse. Choose a greenhouse that is adequately insulated and ventilated to achieve this. When it's cold outside, you should be able to keep your greenhouse warm naturally and heat it if you need to. Keeping your greenhouse cool during the summer months is essential. Allowing for installing additional base vents, exhaust fans, and solar-powered louvers is crucial for reducing overheating in your greenhouse during the summer and spring months. Furthermore, light diffusion helps to keep temperatures low. Solexx greenhouses may be used all year round, regardless of the weather, allowing you to continue your favorite pastime.

2. Find a greenhouse that provides your plants with the right amount of light.

Everyone understands how important sunlight is for plant growth. However, you might be shocked to learn that natural sunlight is not the best light source for plants. Direct sunshine can be harmful to plants. Sunburns in humans are caused by the same powerful rays that destroy your plants. Diffused light, according to studies, is the best light for growth. When plants are grown in diffused light, their development rates increase by 20% to 30% more than when they are grown indirect light.

Plants in places with diffused light receive light from all directions, reducing the amount of shade. Plants will no longer have to strain to reach available light. As a result, your greenhouse plants develop healthy, compact development.

Greenhouse covers have a wide range of light diffusion qualities. In most single-walled greenhouse covering materials, such as glass, the diffusion qualities are almost non-existent. Partially diffused light is provided through polycarbonate greenhouse covers. Due to its 100 percent diffusion, Solexx greenhouse panels provide the most diffuse light available. It doesn't matter if it's cloudy outside. The inside of a Solexx greenhouse is always bright. Solexx is different from other greenhouse cover materials because it lets light shine through the whole structure of the greenhouse.

In the greenhouse, too much light leads to too much heat. Plants lose energy due to this process, which is akin to sweating. Plants are stressed as a result, and their photosynthetic rates are reduced. In fact, in a greenhouse, the heat kills more plants than the cold.

To protect your children and grandchildren from the sun, you would never allow them to play outside without wearing sunscreen beforehand. Nourish your plants with the same level of care and give them the greatest start possible. Solexx greenhouse panels are the finest option to protect your plants.

3. Choose a greenhouse that can adjust to your needs.

Growing plants in a greenhouse is an extremely addictive hobby! As you gain experience with your greenhouse pastime, your demands will likely change as you discover new ways to make the most of it. A good greenhouse should be adjustable and customizable to your specific needs and the climate in which you live. It doesn't matter whether you're boosting greenhouse production by installing additional accessories or expanding your growing space by installing an extension kit; make sure the greenhouse you choose is easily customizable. With the right greenhouse, you can grow everything from tropicals to succulents, flowers to herbs - all in the same place!

4. Find out if the greenhouse provides UV (ultraviolet) protection.

It should be simple to manage your greenhouse. That means you shouldn't waste time restoring the greenhouse over and over again. Greenhouses must be made to endure the harsh direct sunlight and hence be long-lasting. The greenhouse structure and windows are UV-treated to extend their life. Consider selecting a greenhouse that has a UV-damage warranty. Inquire about the pricing of replacement parts as well as their availability.

5. Choose a sturdy and long-lasting greenhouse.

A good greenhouse should handle everyday life and extreme weather conditions. Falling tree limbs, rocks tossed by lawnmowers, and stray baseballs are hazards to greenhouses. Poorly constructed greenhouses can also be harmed by harsh weather such as snow, wind, and hail.

Consider greenhouses with frames that are simple to maintain. Ideally, you'll want something simple to clean, like the Solexx greenhouses' sturdy composite frame. This ensures that any disease or pests that make their way into your greenhouse are removed.

The greenhouse's paneling should be just as tough. Scratch- and impact resistance are both important requirements. If you live in an area where there is a lot of snow or other bad weather, it's vital that your greenhouse cover can handle the extra weight.

6. Select a greenhouse that is simple to maintain.

Cleaning and maintaining your greenhouse should be simple. Consider scratch-resistant, mold- and mildew-resistant, and water-etch-resistant greenhouse materials. Also, bear in mind that some greenhouse coverings have an outside UV protection layer, and you must be careful not to harm it. Find out how much it costs to maintain a greenhouse. You want to keep your greenhouse looking good for as long as possible, so make sure it's appealing and functional.

7. Find a greenhouse with sufficient growing space.

The size of your desired greenhouse should be proportional to the available space and the plants. Remember that irrespective of the size of the greenhouse kit you choose, you will most probably fill it within a year. You'll need a lot of room to expand when you first start.

The size of the greenhouse you'll need is also dictated by the amount of growing space you have available. Growing vertically in Solexx greenhouses is made possible by the greenhouses' built-in bench frames. In addition, the hanging rods allow you to keep your beautiful hanging baskets safe and dry all winter long.

The most important factor to consider when choosing a greenhouse is its performance. Your greenhouse should make growing your favorite plants as simple as possible while still producing exceptional results. To get the most out of your greenhouse, you need to know what kind of climate you're dealing with and what kind of plants you'll be producing. It may be difficult to find a perfect greenhouse for your unique requirements in today's market, where there are so many possibilities. When you know what aspects affect a greenhouse's efficiency, you may be confident that you'll get your desired outcomes.

1.2 Kinds of Greenhouses

Greenhouses provide you a lot more control over the circumstances in which your fruits, vegetables, and other plants are grown; you may grow non-native species of plants that don't flourish in local conditions all year long inside. Though a greenhouse may appear to be nothing more than a glass building, various greenhouses vary in size, accessibility, complexity, and construction cost.

Lean-to Greenhouse

A lean-to greenhouse is a tiny construction that links to an existing house or building and has either a curved roof or a plain roof that links to the eaves of the current building's roof. Lean-to greenhouses often have limited area and no heating or electrical equipment of their own, rather relying on the bigger home's or building's energy and heating. These greenhouses are frequently less expensive than other greenhouse choices because they are merely a partial construction.

Even-Span Greenhouse

It is a full-size greenhouse construction that, like a lean-to, attaches to a building on one end but has a bigger growing surface and support gables. Excess greenhouse space can be created by extending the enclosed end of the greenhouse, and lighting or heating equipment can be hung above your plants using the greenhouse support framework. Some even-span greenhouses have a unique door built into the greenhouse's wall, while others require entry from the building to which the greenhouse is connected. Even-span greenhouses are often the most expensive solution when constructing a greenhouse due to the greater size and support system necessary.

Window-Mount Greenhouse

These little greenhouses, attached to a window frame on a house or other structure, are perfect for growing just a few plants. Mounting these greenhouses on the north or west side of a structure results in the greenhouse being in the shade for most of the day. This is why these small greenhouses are often put on a home or building's west or north side to ensure they receive enough light.

Gutter-Connected Greenhouse

These greenhouses can be free-standing or connected to an existing structure in the same way that even-span greenhouses are. The greenhouse comprises several interconnected greenhouse sections, each with a furrow or gutter connecting its roofing gables to provide proper rainwater drainage. Internal walls are frequently eliminated to provide room for more people, though walls with doors can divide each portion into its own greenhouse space with its temperature control.

Free-Standing Greenhouse

Free-standing greenhouses are self-contained constructions that do not require attachment to an existing structure. Because there is no associated building from which electrical lines or hoses can flow, these greenhouses can be constructed as smaller or larger as needed. They also require their separate water, electricity, and heating solutions. A free-standing greenhouse for optimal lighting for your plants allows you greater flexibility when placing your greenhouse for optimal lighting.

Construction Materials

Greenhouses can be constructed from a variety of materials. The structure of a greenhouse can be made of aluminum, steel, or treated wood, with aluminum being the most cost-effective alternative. Fiberglass, glass or multiple layers of polyethylene film can be used to make greenhouse covering panels. Glass transmits more light than the other options, but it is more expensive and requires a larger structure to hold it; fiberglass is lightweight and less expensive, but it does not allow as much light to pass through and then becomes brittle with time when exposed to UV light. Polyethylene film is inexpensive, lightweight, and does not grow brittle when exposed to UV light, although it must be renewed every two years due to its thin nature.

1.3 Create Greenhouse Environment

With the correct greenhouse and knowledge, you can turn your grow space into the ideal environment for growing just about any crop - and even boost the yield of those you've been growing for years.

Few elements have a greater impact on your overall production than effective environmental control when it comes to growing your best plants in your greenhouse. However, maintaining the optimum conditions for your crops in your greenhouse can be difficult, especially if you don't know what to look for.

Here's a look at some of the most critical environmental aspects affecting your greenhouse crops, as well as what you can do to ensure your plants are in the best possible environment to produce the best harvest yet.

Factors

Any scientist will tell you that air temperature is only one aspect of a growing environment. It's a complex mix of elements that drive plant growth, with the four most important being heat, humidity, light, and ventilation.

You have a higher probability of producing exactly the appropriate mix - or "environment" - for your plants to grow than ever before if you understand each of these aspects and take control of them individually.

Humidity

Humidity, which is closely linked to temperature and can significantly impact the conditions in your greenhouse if left unregulated, is also critical for crop success.

Humidity has long been left to nature on outside fields, where it can be very changeable due to rain or drought, but it now plays a vital part in greenhouse environmental controls. As plants grow and consume CO_2, they naturally exhale warm, moist oxygen into the air, making your greenhouse humid and warmer over time.

While some plants thrive in a slightly damp atmosphere (think tomatoes, cucumbers, and other water-rich vegetables), too much moisture can promote the growth of ugly molds and even host pests or diseases, all of which can cause irreversible damage to your crops without warning.

You can closely track and monitor the moisture in your greenhouse using a mix of correct airflow and heat management to ensure everything is precisely where it should be to limit mold formation while boosting plant growth.

Heat

Some crops just can't stand the heat, while others may thrive in it. Delivering the ideal temperature for your fruits, leafy greens, vegetables, and flowers.

If you ask any greenhouse gardener in a cooler climate where the hottest spot on their field is, they'll almost certainly direct you to the greenhouse itself. Plants produce heat as they "breathe" CO_2 and expel oxygen, a warm, wet heat that may quickly build up if left unattended. Tomatoes, peas, peppers, and avocados, which thrive in warm environments, can benefit from this heat buildup, which can act as a natural heat source to protect your plants when the temperature outside your greenhouse is chilly.

Similarly, greenhouse temperature controls assist you in cooling down your greenhouse during the warmer months, when an abundance of heat can cause extreme heat and other high-temperature diseases, reducing your output.

Shade coverings, UV-resistant poly, and proper ventilation can all help keep your greenhouse's inside temperature low enough for your plants to thrive.

Sunlight

Though growers working in open fields under the bare sun have long had little control over sunlight, the skill to choose your greenhouse protective cover to monitor and control sunlight levels - and even filter out Ultraviolet rays while keeping light levels high - has had a huge impact on growers all over the world looking at expanding their growing seasons.

Almost every farmer is aware that some plants love full sun while others prefer some shade, but never before has it been so simple for a grower to supply both possibilities on the same plot of land.

Growers may fine-tune their plants' light diet with unprecedented degrees of control by using equipment like black-out curtains, shade coverings, energy curtains, and UV-filtering plastic or poly covers.

Ventilation

Ventilation has long been an uncontrolled issue in outdoor horticulture, whether in the breezy plains of the midwest or the still deserts of the southeast. However, because of advancements in greenhouse technology, farmers now have complete control over their ventilation efforts, which means you no longer have to wait for the perfect breeze to keep your crops growing strong.

Ventilation is critical for everything from temperature adjustment to humidity control, and consistent airflow might be critical for giving fresh CO_2 to indoor plants.

For most modern growers, appropriate ventilation may be accomplished using a mix of vents and fans placed directly into the greenhouse wall. By promoting airflow on calm days and closing gaps on windy days, you may more naturally manage temperature, add or remove moisture, and keep plants supplied with breathing CO_2 all year.

1.4 Basic Greenhouse Accessories

When you first start your gardening hobby, you will require a few essential accessories. Perhaps not a complete greenhouse, but most certainly seeds, pots, and trays. As for greenhouse accessories, you'll always need a few essentials. If you do not already have these, continue reading for greenhouse accessories to explore. If you already have them, keep reading to learn about greenhouse equipment.

The following are the essential items you'll need to start cultivating plants.

Seedboxes

Seedboxes are also a necessary piece of greenhouse equipment.

Plastic seedboxes are displacing the wood boxes that many gardeners previously used.

The advantages and disadvantages of wood vs. plastic continue to be argued globally. Avoid plastic and stick to wood if you truly want to go green.

Purchase seedboxes, however, that measure approximately fourteen inches X eight inches X two inches. This is an ideal size for growing tiny seeds.

Greenhouse containers

Your selection of greenhouse containers is critical since it has a significant impact on the growth of your vegetables or plants. Gardeners can use nearly anything that holds soil in greenhouse planters as long as it fits these two characteristics. They ought to:

- Promote good health by providing ample root area and appropriate drainage.
- Maintain a firm grip on the crop and control its upward growth.

Containers come in various shapes and sizes, including plugs and flats, pots and hanging baskets. Additionally, larger containers are available suited to store a variety of smaller pots. Hanging baskets are ideal for growing plants, flowers, and vegetables vertically and efficiently. They are available in various materials, including plastic, metal, ceramic, and even coconut fiber. Plugs and flat pots are widely utilized to facilitate early germination.

These containers are ideal for containing a variety of miniature flowers or plants while maintaining their separation. Gardeners prefer clay greenhouse pots because they are the traditional method of producing flowers and plants for potting. If you cannot purchase clay pots, you can also use wood, plastic, peat moss, and wood fiber. These are frequently lighter, durable, and less expensive than clay pots. Additionally, they are simply disposed of.

Selecting greenhouse and nursery containers and pots

The soil is porous greenhouse containers can quickly dry out, necessitating more frequent watering. In non-porous pots, the soil retains moisture more effectively, avoiding over-watering. When selecting greenhouse containers and pots, keep in mind that they should provide more than just adequate growth space for plants; they should also provide adequate drainage and porosity.

In general, if you intend to grow crops year-round, you must plan for mobility. Your greenhouse pots should be lightweight and easily transportable. You'll want to ensure that your containers are environmentally friendly, which will provide the best possible habitat for your plant. When greenhouse supplies and pots are used properly, it is possible to grow baby plants from seedlings even when the soil is incompatible with germination. Choosing the appropriate greenhouse container makes a significant difference in the overall growth of your greenhouse plants.

Watering can

You may also want to consider purchasing a watering bucket and a greenhouse plant mister. These items will make watering plants a breeze. Using a watering can with a small tip assists in preventing soil movement. You can purchase one made of plastic or metal.

Plastic cans are often lighter than metal cans, which makes watering easier. Additionally, they are frequently less expensive. A little sprayer will assist you in misting plants to provide more moisture. Regardless of whether you intend to install a greenhouse irrigation system, you need to have these accessories.

Heavy pots

Additionally, you should examine the weight of your pots. On greenhouse shelves, you require lightweight pots. Utilizing larger pots on the ground closer to the greenhouse walls will assist in securing the greenhouse in the event of a windstorm.

With a greenhouse, that is, you'll fix it in place with stakes or something like cinder blocks. Additionally, adding hefty pots can assist. Keep large pots on the ground rather than on greenhouse shelves to avoid shattering.

Soil test kits

If you notice a plant is suffering or does not appear to be as healthy as previously, you can do a soil test.

You may obtain a soil test kit to determine the phosphorus, nitrogen, and potassium levels in your soil (NPK). These tests are simple to use and provide reliable results for any deficiencies in the soil.

Moisture meter

Light and moisture meter is another inexpensive greenhouse accessory. This tool you insert into the soil to determine the plant's moisture level. You can adjust the setting to choose the amount of light. What's good about these simple-to-use meters is that they can test for light, moisture, and soil pH.

1.5 Seed Starting

Greenhouses are common to start seeds in open flat seed trays or individual plug trays. Seeds can be soaked overnight, stratified or scarified, and then planted in trays in the greenhouse, according to the species' needs. To make fertilizing, watering, thinning, and treating seedling ailments like damping off easier, seeds are often planted in tidy rows in open flat trays. After the seedlings have sprouted their first true leaves, they are placed in individual pots or cells. To avoid overcrowding, single-cell trays only allow for the planting of one or two seeds per cell. Because plug cells absorb and store more heat and moisture for developing seeds, planting in plug trays is preferred by many experts over open trays. The roots of the seedlings in plug trays do not get entangled with those of the neighbors; thus, they can be left there longer. Plants can be transplanted from plug-grown seedlings into a garden or container arrangement. You don't need to buy expensive seed starting mixtures in a greenhouse. Peat moss, perlite and organic material can be combined in an all-purpose potting mix to save money on commercial products (such as compost). To avoid the seedling illness known as damping off, it's vital to disinfect all potting material in between usage. If the greenhouse temperature is too low, the light is too dim, or the seedlings are overwatered, they may develop lanky, weak stems.

Begin with a new seed, or test the germination of last year's leftover seed before using it. You can either put 10 or 100 seeds on a damp paper towel. Store the seeds in a plastic bag with the damp paper folded over them and warm them. Keep an eye on things twice a day by taking the paper off and sprinkling the seeds with water as needed. Count the germinated seeds and calculate the germination percentage after the usual number of days for that variety.

GREENHOUSE GARDENING FOR BEGINNERS

Planning

Your Greenhouse seedlings will require a full-sun to part-sun position year-round, depending on the climate in your area. Greenhouses are available in various sizes and styles to fit any outdoor location, from balconies to backyards. There's no need for any fasteners or anything. This is a terrific activity for the whole family to work on together!

The climate in your area should be considered while deciding where to place the Greenhouse. Some shade or protection is needed in hotter cities, where temperatures might reach over 30oF. This prevents your seedlings from becoming too hot. We recommend securing the floor of your Greenhouse to the ground in coastal or windy areas. To keep it from blowing over in high winds, anchor it with a large, heavy object like a pot or a brick.

Growing Media

Before sowing, test the growing medium for soluble salts and pH both on-site and at a soil testing facility. Most crops benefit from seed germination conditions with a pH of 5.6 to 6.3 and minimal soluble salts. Soluble salts and pH cause many seedling issues. Irrigation water should also be tested by sending samples to a commercial laboratory.

Sowing

When using plug trays, the position of the seed is crucial. To avoid desiccation, seeds should be placed towards the cell's perimeter.

Vermiculite should be used to create a high-humidity microenvironment while covering the seed. Fine vermiculite can cause the seed to be buried. Lightly covered or uncovered seedlings need sunlight to germinate. Keep things moist with a misting device.

If the seed is little, be extra careful when watering plug flats to avoid burying them. If the seed is kept moist, it is more likely that plug germination will succeed or fail. Temperature and moisture requirements are determined by the type of crop being cultivated. Between waterings, the growing media can be let to dry out slightly.

Once seeds have been sown, place them in an area with adequate humidity and water to ensure germination. It can be used to categorize crops depending on their temperature needs. Staying in the same place where you sowed your seeds for a long time can disturb the seeds by dryness.

Germination is more successful when seeds are sprouted in germination chambers or on a bench exposed to warm temperatures and consistent moisture. Commercially available germination chamber systems include both pre-fabricated and custom-built options. Growers widely use root zone heating or bottom heat to maintain a consistent temperature in the root zone. The benchtop is covered with hot water-filled rubber tubing or carpets. On top of the bench, a weed mat barrier is put, with skirts on each side to assist contain the heat. As soon as radicles sprout through the seed coat, remove flats from the germination box. Experimentation and expertise are the keys to a successful seeding process.

When using a germination chamber, it is vital to maintain the ideal humidity level until the trays are placed on the bench.

Containers

Transplants can be grown in a wide variety of containers. Sowing seeds is done on open seed flats or single-cell (plug) trays. Whether the seeds will be sown in one container and finished in another before sowing or if they will be sown in one container and finished in a different container before sowing.

Growers commonly use open seed flats for row planting. It is less difficult to control damping-off disease in seedlings. If the seed is sown too thickly, the seedlings will be cramped, resulting in stretched plants and high humidity around the seedlings, which favors damping-off diseases and makes transplanting difficult.

Many gardeners make use of plug trays for a variety of different plants. Studies have shown that the medium's oxygenation and drainage were improved by using plug trays with deeper columns. When it comes to germination, the depth of the plug tray isn't as critical as maintaining the correct humidity and temperature.

Lighting

Seedlings should be positioned near a window as feasible if grown inside. Suppose you're growing seedlings in a greenhouse; attempt to place them in a spot that gets the most light. Many farmers start seeds in a greenhouse or indoors using an artificial light source. If you've seen seedlings with leggy, stretched stems, you've seen the effects of insufficient illumination. A light source placed above the seedlings will make them healthy and compact. Numerous artificial light sources are available for seedlings, but T5 fluorescents are particularly effective and relatively inexpensive. A light for seed beginning is an extremely useful item worth the cost.

Planting seeds in a greenhouse or inside is a fun and easy way to get a jump on the growing season. Hobbyists who sow their seeds at the correct time while also providing suitable atmospheric conditions, medium, and illumination will have increased germination efficiency and have many healthy seedlings prepared to take on the forthcoming growing season.

Fertilizing

The fertilizer used will impact the type of plant growth and the pH of the media. Fertilizers derived from peat moss (such as 20-10-20) have a lower pH and promote more shoot growth than other types of fertilizer. Fertilizers like 13(nitrate)-2(phosphorus)-13[minors][nitrate] have been found by most farmers to improve root health and pH balance in the soil.

Media EC levels should be monitored to prevent excessive soluble salts, which injure roots and cause root rot from accumulating. Seedlings are often started on a low-nitrogen fertilizer program (25-50 ppm N) at the second stage (cotyledon opening), and as they grow and approach transplanting, the dosage is gradually increased.

Rinse fertilizer from growing tips and delicate new leaves before applying it on sunny days. Plants vulnerable to this disease include salvia, ageratum, coleus, and snapdragons.

Chapter 2
Greenhouse Equipment

2.1 Greenhouse Drainage And Irrigation Equipment

Installing a greenhouse irrigation system is something you should consider if you have a walk-in greenhouse. In addition to saving you time, irrigation systems can help your plants get the nutrients they need. A greenhouse irrigation kit can be purchased, or you can create your own.

It will be easier with irrigation systems because you may alter the system according to the season and the requirements of the plants. Your greenhouse can be watered continuously using a drip irrigation system, or you can set it up to be hosed off once a day or less often.

While automated plant watering devices are useful, watering cans will always be special in traditional gardening practices. They will be able to reach all of your crops, even those who are at the end of the garden, thanks to their long spouts.

GREENHOUSE GARDENING FOR BEGINNERS

Greenhouse Accessories

Heavy planters are an excellent greenhouse accessory to consider. Keep them on the floor near the greenhouse's walls. Their heaviness will help to keep the greenhouse stable in the wind. You should avoid keeping heavy pots on greenhouse racks during adverse weather, such as rainstorms. Think about these greenhouse accessories regardless of the size of your greenhouse.

- Basics
- Seed starters
- Potting soil
- Greenhouse furniture
- Soil and pH test kits
- Moisture meter
- Planters, tray, pots
- Light meter
- Watering can

Greenhouse Equipment

Having the best greenhouse accessories and greenhouse equipment might be critical to properly operating a greenhouse. Your choices will be determined by the sort of greenhouse you own. The more space you have within the greenhouse, the more you can do. If you possess a walk-in greenhouse, for example, you may be able to install greenhouse equipment such as grow lights, irrigation, and extra ventilation.

You may simply require greenhouse accessories such as a humidity meter and soil sample testing kits for a compact greenhouse that may sit on a patio. The purpose of having a greenhouse is to cultivate plants regardless of the environment or conditions. There is equipment available to help you do so.

Controlling the interior humidity and temperature levels is one of them. Consider putting in a water line inside your house so that you may use it for irrigation or simply because it's handier. Keep in mind that the bigger your greenhouse, the more you can accomplish with growing lights, space for greenhouse supplies, planting a variety of plants, and so on.

Greenhouse Equipment:

- Water management
- Lighting
- Ventilation
- Heating
- Climate control

- Pest control

When building greenhouses, each of these components must be considered.

2.2 Furniture To Store Your Plants And Greenhouse Equipment

Well-planned furniture and appropriate shelving within a greenhouse will accommodate all your pots and containers.

Bench For Greenhouse Storage

Garden benches are one type of shelving that maximizes storage and space. The width of the hothouse often decides its optimal size to maximize growing space. Benches can be permanent or temporary structures, making them useful greenhouse accents.

If you want to rearrange or remove them regularly, sectioned bench alternatives may be advantageous. Greenhouse benches significantly enhance the appearance of a greenhouse.

Greenhouse shelves

Shelving can increase the growing surface in a compact greenhouse with limited space without impairing the shade. Certain greenhouse shelves are movable (on wheels) and may be moved outside during the day and then returned inside at night or during periods of cold weather. Shelves can be made of wood, glass, or metal. It's critical to keep in mind that when double shelving is employed, the amount of light reaching the plants may be reduced. Additionally, shelves under garden benches can be used to save space. Greenhouse shelves can be temporary, connected to the greenhouse frame, or permanent, used to start seedlings. Cinder, woodblocks, and metal are excellent materials for the shelves' legs and stands. The shelves' wire meshes allow excess water to drain away. Additionally, greenhouse shelving can assist in separating crops to minimize seeding or cross-pollination.

Planters For Storage

Planters are another form of greenhouse gardening item. You can store greenhouse equipment such as shovels, hoes, gardening gloves, rakes, and spades in nursery pots and heavy-duty planters. You can secure them and make them easily accessible by using hefty planters made of clay, ceramic, or other materials.

Chapter 3
Greenhouse Plants

3.1 Beginners' Guide to Growing Easy Greenhouse Plants

For many yards, a greenhouse is practically feasible. Numerous individuals like these indoor environments due to the controlled environment. For instance, the watering system's automatic timing. It enables you to save time and maintain environmental control regardless of the season or time of day.

Automatic ventilation regulates the airflow within the room. It provides a continuous supply of carbon dioxide to your greenhouse plants. They need this for the creation of sugar and oxygen. Carbon dioxide concentration results in larger leaves and more vigorous plant stems. Additionally, it enhances the likelihood of early blooming and fruiting. Greenhouses with moisture regulators maintain an ideal humidity level for optimal plant development. Every plant can concentrate on blossoming and fruiting in a humid environment. Additionally, moist soil is less prone to harbor pests and illnesses.

Fundamentals that can still affect the growth of plants even in a greenhouse

There are several things to keep in mind that can still affect your plants' growth. Several of them you are probably already familiar with from your outside gardening.

pH level

The most fundamental reason that gardeners may ignore is a soil pH level that is either too high or too low. It can inhibit germination even if no apparent indicators are present. If you haven't been tracking the pH, you should immediately determine if this is the main cause of your trouble! Some of your plants may have an unbalanced pH level at the roots. This is very likely to occur even though they are in a similar environment.

GREENHOUSE GARDENING FOR BEGINNERS

Water

Underwatering or overwatering are frequently cited reasons for seedling growth delays. Typically, this is followed by wilting or drooping. Certain plants absorb more naturally than others. The amount of sufficient water for one plant may be excessive for another. Keep a tight eye on your watering when a seedling is growing slowly.

Finding the optimal watering frequency for greenhouse rookies can be challenging at first. It retains moisture for a longer period than a garden, but you also lose reliance on rain. Additionally, you can organize your greenhouse plants as per their water requirements to keep track of them.

Seeds

Planting using old seeds is possible. However, you may be wondering the odds of germinating them. Let us look at these three important elements that can affect your seeds' viability.

- **Age**

    Each seed is active for at least one year, and some are viable for two. However, after their first year, out-of-date seeds' germination percentages decline.

- **Storage**

If handled properly, older packets may have a better chance of preserving the seeds. Seeds will last far longer if stored in a cold, dark area. Your refrigerator's vegetable drawer is an excellent storage choice.

Easy To Grow Greenhouse Vegetables

Vegetables are the most popular crops to raise. A year-round supply of organic vegetables is ideal, and greenhouses can contribute to this healthy lifestyle.

Green onions

Green onions grow rapidly in a chilly, coastal region or a temperature-controlled greenhouse. They are among the easiest crops to grow and require little maintenance. Onions are a popular choice for starter plants. Ideal for beginning greenhouse gardeners. Seedlings can be started indoors and then transplanted outside.

It can be grown from sets or seeds. The simplest approach to begin is to develop them from sets. Onion sets are advantageous since they flourish in all conditions, including chilly greenhouses.

Plant the bulbs directly into well-drained soil. Once the onions get established in your greenhouse, they require regular watering. Do this even more so when the weather is hot. When the plants have swollen, it is advisable to stop watering them. It is safe to uproot when the foliage turns yellow and dies back. Following that, they should be dried in the sun. What could be simpler?

They are more resistant to pests and illness. Before adding soil to your flats and containers, sanitize them with a 10% bleach solution to reduce disease risk.

Carrots

Carrots are among the most widely grown root crops due to their ease of planting. They can be planted at any time of year, even in the winter. There is no need to be concerned because it is frost resistant. If you're concerned about growing carrots, fear not. Simply create a soil that is loose, sandy, heavily tilled, and loose. This will allow them to plunge without feeling any pressure. Ascertain that it is not excessively thick. Otherwise, you will end up producing carrots that are undersized and spherical!

Regrettably, no pesticides have been registered to control common carrot pests and illnesses. The great news is that most of them have already developed resistance to most pests and diseases. Conduct a thorough examination of the packages. Sow only disease-free seeds. Regular soil work can overcome these impediments.

Additionally, harvesting earlier than anticipated is OK. This is only possible if the damage occurs late in maturity. Crop rotation with non-susceptible plants for three years is recommended. Ensure that infectious residue is discarded and destroyed.

Carrots require between two and four months to mature. It is dependent on the kind and growing conditions. Certain types may take an additional few weeks. Typically, they are ready after about 75 days. Pulling frequently results in a handful of leaves. However, there are no carrots connected. Before harvesting carrots, loosen the soil using a garden fork.

Spinach

Spinach is a cold-weather, tough-as-nails green vegetable. It is a widespread crop that may be produced all year. The majority of spinach grows in cool climates. Pests are rarely a problem, even for a novice.

They thrive in similar conditions to lettuce but are more nutritious. It can be consumed raw or cooked. It has more iron, calcium, and vitamins than other grown vegetables. It is also a good source of vitamins.

GREENHOUSE GARDENING FOR BEGINNERS

Spinach loves broad sun to mild shade with well-drained soil. Around one week before planting, amend your soil with old manure. Temperatures in the soil should not exceed 70oF. Transplanting seedlings is difficult. This is why starting it indoors is not recommended. Feed them only as necessary. When seedlings reach a couple of inches in height, thin them to a spacing of three to four inches. Mulch the soil to keep it moist.

You can begin harvesting the leaves as soon as they reach an edible stage. Only the outer leaves should be removed. Allow the center leaves to grow in size. This will allow the plant to grow. Additionally, this strategy will temporarily delay bolting.

Asparagus

Are you searching for vegetables that will yield for a minimum of twenty years? Asparagus from the garden is the solution to it. It is best planted from a crown that is one or two years old. Twenty asparagus stems can provide enough asparagus for a four-person household. Asparagus despises rivalry. It is critical to eradicating all weeds and grasses from the area. Never grow other plants in the same location.

Typically, asparagus is planted in a trench. It should be approximately 11 to 13 inches beneath. Enrich the soil with substantial organic materials dug from the trench. Individually position the crowns 12 inches apart, with the shoots pointing upward. You are not required to select everything. If everything is chopped, the crown may perish. Leave a few spears, ideally the smallest. If desired, you can even plant asparagus in deep containers. Avoid being overly thrilled about your first crop. For the first few years, avoid taking too much from it. They must establish a solid root system and gather the energy required.

Turnips

Turnips are a type of mustard green that grows in cooler climates. They are fairly rapid growers. Both the greens and the roots are delectable. Another remarkable feature of this vegetable is that it sprouts in a matter of days. This root crop is adaptable and extremely nutritious to a wide range of climates.

Before seeding, prepare a compost mixture. Turnip seeds are sown directly in the soil. They are not well suited for transplantation. Assure that they have a permanent sunny spot. They do not demand a great deal of attention. However, consistent soil moisture is required.

Never grow turnips in the same location to aid with disease resistance. Crop rotation is necessary. Additionally, floating row covers help protect your plants from pests. Pests are rarely a problem in greenhouses because they mature swiftly and are picked immediately. If you notice an issue, it is already time to harvest.

Within a month, you can already taste the freshness of their greens. The following month, the swollen roots can be picked. Turnips in their infancy are extremely delicate. You may simply peel and eat them like an apple.

Eggplants

Aubergine is another name for eggplant. These warm-weather greens, like peppers and tomatoes, require somewhat warm conditions. Raised beds combined with composted manure provide an ideal environment for eggplants to thrive. The beds will immediately warm the soil.

Once loaded with ripe fruits, eggplants tend to tumble over. Stake them to a height of around 24in. Additionally, you can use a box to keep them upright. Consider some planters and trellis-supported raised beds.

To avoid disease, use the finest potting mix. After planting, thoroughly water them. Apply a layer of mulch to help retain moisture and control weeds. Cut the terminal buds to create a more robust shrub. This vegetable is great for pots and creates visually appealing decorative borders. Harvest between

16 and 24 weeks after sowing, when the skin is bright and wrinkle-free. Avoid removing the eggplant. Cut the fruit close to the stem, leaving about an inch intact.

Easy To Grow Greenhouse Fruits

Strawberries

Strawberry is among the most often grown greenhouse fruits in the United States. Strawberries cultivated in greenhouses have a superior flavor than those purchased at the grocery. Additionally, growing them in a greenhouse reduces disease and pest damage. Additionally, you may like to bring bumblebees inside your greenhouse to aid in pollination. Additionally, you can utilize a rechargeable VegiBee garden pollinator. Ensure that you only purchase disease-free seedlings from reputable nursery retailers. Strawberry cultivation does not have to be complicated. Simply ensure that you follow the simple instructions for growing it.

Strawberries should be planted in pots with a high organic matter content. They require soil that drains well. Mulch helps maintain a constant temperature in the soil. Drip watering is required due to their shallow roots. Pests and diseases may result from sprinkling them from above.

Maintain a clean and healthy greenhouse at all times. Keep an eye out for signs of diseases and pests to avert escalating problems. Strawberries, like raspberries, are susceptible to verticillium wilt. This can be avoided by purchasing variety from reputable retailers. Separate them from other plants, particularly tomatoes.

Tomatoes

Tomatoes are simple to plant outdoors and even simpler in a greenhouse! Nothing compares to having a constant supply of organic tomatoes throughout the year. First, select a variety that is resistant to diseases such as fusarium and verticillium.

Tomatoes are warm-weather plants that cannot tolerate chilly temperatures. Inadequate light can cause plants to appear pale and fragile. There are numerous variations available. Selecting the best type might be challenging. Choose the sort of tomato you wish to use. Take into account the size of fully grown tomatoes about the size of your intended garden.

Ensure that your seeds are planted in well-drained soil. Moisture should be added to the soil but not completely submerged. The optimal temperature range is between 70°F and 75°F. One seedling per container will ensure a robust and vigorous tomato plant. Do not be afraid to thin the plant; it is necessary. Once you see the 2nd set of genuine leaves, begin fertilizing.

Organic tomatoes include a higher concentration of Lycopene. Lycopene aids in the unclogging of clogged arteries. Additionally, it is beneficial to the heart. Another advantage of producing your tomatoes is the incredible variety of sizes, shapes, colors, and flavors.

Raspberries

Raspberries may be cultivated year-round in a greenhouse. They are easy to cultivate and can provide fruit consistently. Primocane blooms and yields fruit all in the same year. They can bear fruit within their first year of maturity. Floricanes have one-year-old stems that mature into fruit and blooms. They are typically summer fruiting varieties.

They require no additional light and develop normally in practically dark settings. A temperature of 70°F in the greenhouse is ideal for growth. Raspberry canes should be purchased from a reputable garden source. Set up a drip irrigation system for planted raspberries to avoid rot caused by overhead watering. The harvest season lasts approximately eight to ten weeks. Do not store them for an extended period. You might want to consider freezing a few for later use. Arrange them on a dish and freeze. Once frozen, transfer them to freezer bags.

Cherries

Cherries are a type of fruit that may be grown in greenhouses. Potted cherries require less greenhouse space and are easily moved. Cherry types that do not require cross-pollination are the most straightforward to grow.

They would fruit similarly to outdoors if the water, temperature, soil, and nutrients were optimal. Once a year, fertilize your cherry trees. Ascertain that your greenhouse is adequately ventilated. Prevent the temperature from rapidly rising, especially during the summer. Pruning it lightly with scissors is recommended. Eliminate any broken or dead branches. Prevent disease outbreaks by optimizing airflow, trimming, and routine cleaning. Leave no leaves or rotting fruits on the ground.

While we understand your excitement about harvesting your cherries, you will need a great deal of patience. Harvesting them prematurely may result in the spoilage of your fruit. It will take up to three years to bear fruit.

Grapes

You are correct! You do not need a vineyard to cultivate your delectable grapes. They are not nearly as demanding as they appear in terms of growth. Watering, training, fertilizing, and pruning require only a minimal amount of attention. It is possible to maintain a consistent crop year after year.

Greenhouse vines should be planted on the other edge of the greenhouse from the entry. The stems were trained along the greenhouse's side, parallel to the roof's ridge, and near the door. You can begin it outside or inside with the root for larger greenhouses. Throughout the growing stage, water them every seven to ten days.

When the greenhouse grapevine matures into bloom, it may require some assistance with pollination. As these curling tendrils appear, remove them. They will simply become entangled in the fruits. Allow the vines to grow wild rather than following your training and pruning regimen. You can even improve your chances of harvesting a good crop. One vine is sufficient to cover the bottom of a tub for smaller greenhouses.

Easy To Grow Greenhouse Flowers

Plant your flowers in a greenhouse to experience spring, even in the dead of winter. These easy-to-grow flowers will undoubtedly create the ideal mood. Take a break and enjoy gardening!

African violets

African violets are extremely easy to care for and often bloom throughout the long winter months. They are one of the most aesthetically pleasing flowers. This perennial favorite blooms on many occasions throughout the year.

African violets prefer a warm atmosphere (not exceeding 85°F and not falling below 65°F). You can maintain it blooming in bright yet indirect sunlight with wet soil. They can flourish well without natural light if the days are too short. Proper drainage and a fortnightly application of African violet fertilizer can assist.

Bear in mind that if the soil is too dry or there is little light, the plant may produce fewer or no flowers. Avoid using cold water as it will develop stains on the foliage.

Marigold

African violets are extremely easy to care for and often bloom throughout the long winter months. They are one of the most aesthetically pleasing flowers. This perennial favorite blooms on many occasions throughout the year.

African violets prefer a warm atmosphere (not exceeding 85°F and not falling below 65°F). You can maintain it blooming in bright yet indirect sunlight with wet soil. They can flourish well without natural light if the days are too short. Proper drainage and a fortnightly application of African violet fertilizer can assist. Bear in mind that if the soil is too dry or there is little light, the plant may produce fewer or no flowers. Avoid using cold water as it will develop stains on the foliage.

Kalanchoe

Kalanchoe blossfeldiana is among the most well-known greenhouse potted flowers. The rich stem-tip cuttings are nearly effortless to grow. Postharvest output is quite impressive. It produces blooms that bloom for an extended period and serve as an exquisite adornment for your greenhouse or home. They are day-length-restricted plants. It blooms when the length of the day is equal to or less than twelve hours.

In autumn, winter, and early spring, many flowering potted plants are grown. This is when the real levels of light are low.

GREENHOUSE GARDENING FOR BEGINNERS

This water-retentive shrub blooms with vibrant bell-shaped flowers. Additionally, it requires very little upkeep. Kalanchoe thrives in arid climates and with temperature swings. It's also rather pleasant in the winter, with a temperature of 45°F.

Daisies

The majority of gardeners appreciate their easy-to-grow nature. They seem to grow in an infinite variety of shapes and sizes.

Daisies are often grown from seeds. Healthy soil is necessary for planting the majority of flowers. Fertile and well-draining soil is required. Trimming and deadheading regularly is necessary to keep them blossoming.

Pests and illnesses rarely wreak havoc on daisies. In most cases, they do not need insecticides. In rare instances where diseases and pests are an issue, you can treat them using a bar of insecticidal soap at the first indication of trouble.

Plant in full light and water thoroughly but not excessively. This will result in them being excessively tall and slim, necessitating staking. They will seek the sunlight and fall over if they are in a shaded area.

Sunflowers

Almost everyone's favorite. You will undoubtedly be mesmerized by the sunflowers that reach a height of ten feet! Distribute the seeds in a sunny, protected location and watch them grow.

Sunflower seeds germinate swiftly when started in greenhouses before the growing season. Allow these sun-loving flowers at least 10 to 13 hours of direct sunlight per day. Additionally, you can supply artificial light if natural daylight is insufficient to satisfy them.

Slugs and snails adore young, growing plants. Use a covering defense, such as the top of a plastic bottle, to shield them. As the sunflower develops and grows taller, you may wish to hold it straight up. To achieve the best results, string a stick to the stem.

Easy To Grow Greenhouse Herbs & Spices

Herbs for medicinal and culinary purposes are now available daily. These easy-to-grow herbs are certain to get you started in gardening.

Cilantro

Cilantro grows nicely in containers and well-prepared gardens with loose, well-draining soil. This herb can grow to a height of three feet. They are extremely easy to grow and self-seed.

This herb requires regular watering. They thrive in full sun and loose soil that has been amended with organic matter. In warm conditions, they will blossom and go to seed shortly. Avoid transplanting them. The lengthy taproot is extremely delicate, and if damaged, the plant will die. At temperatures ranging from 51°F to 84°F, the seeds grow. It often occurs within seven to ten days.

Remove any dead leaves and debris from the ground. Wash the leaves sometimes to disrupt the normal spore-releasing cycle. PM wash and neem oil can halt a fungal invasion on a seven-day timetable. Apply organic compost that is slow to decompose. Never apply nitrogen that is not essential. As needed, harvest fresh leaves. Cilantro is gathered best in the early morning. Avoid washing the leaves since this will remove the fragrance oils.

Mint

Mint is easy to cultivate due to its vibrant and invasive properties. Mint sends lateral root runners under the soil surface. It will also manifest in other areas of your neighborhood. They compete for light, water, and nutrients with other plants simultaneously.

Mint should be planted around 2 inches beneath and 12 inches apart. It should be well-watered. Using settling boards, determine the roots' proclivity to reach surrounding plant roots. Bricks 1 foot deep can be laid throughout beds. Additionally, you can bury it in a large, deep plastic container dug into your plant bed. Additionally, you can use a container or pot elevated above the soil or on a shelf.

If you find any evidence of mint rust, remove and destroy them immediately. They spread rapidly to other soil and plants. It will soon impact new crops. Mint leaves can make tea or as a garnish for cold beverages. Spearmint is frequently utilized in the production of mint flavorings and jellies. Before cooking, sprinkle raw or dried leaves over plain lamb. Savor the unique flavor!

Sage

Sage is an easy plant to produce from seeds. We recommend pairing this hardy perennial with other herbs such as rosemary and basil to get a head start. Seedlings cultivated in a greenhouse can be planted about one foot apart.

Slugs and Spider mites are two common pests found on sage. Remove weeds and other garden debris. Place severely affected plants in the garbage.

Throughout the 1st year of growth, harvest the leaves cautiously. Select as necessary during the next few years. While sage is best when consumed fresh, it can also be preserved. Dried leaves have a strong, slightly distinct flavor than fresh leaves.

Sage leaves, dried, are a classic component of bird stuffing. When the flowers become brown and dry, the seeds are ready for collection. When the heads are completely dry, lightly crush them and carefully extract the waste.

Thyme

Thymes are relatively simple plants to produce from seed. Germination can take between 14 and 28 days. Seedlings are best started indoors, where a temperature of roughly 70°F can be maintained. As a result, a greenhouse is an ideal location for it. Sow seeds in shallow rows approximately one foot apart. After stabilizing your seedlings, thin them to six inches apart.

Thyme should be harvested before the blossoms begin to open. Cut the herb one and a half to two inches from the site. A 2nd growth will appear, which should not be clipped. This would have a detrimental effect on the plant's winter hardiness. Even though it is a hardy perennial, it does require some maintenance over the winter months to survive the chilly environment.

3.2 Growing Vegetable Herbs, And Fruit

A greenhouse can be used to extend the growing season and allow you to enjoy fresh and organic fruits, vegetables, and herbs for a much longer period of the year, or it can be heated to allow year-round growing. Greenhouses can be self-contained structures built in a sunny location or modest enclosures attached to an existing exterior wall. Whichever design you choose, keep in mind that producing vegetables in a greenhouse is not the same as growing them outdoors. Prepare to devote slightly more attention to your greenhouse plants than you would to plants growing outdoors.

Temperature Control

Air vents, screens, shade cloths, and vinyl netting are used to cool greenhouses. Additionally, an evaporative cooler may be required. Make sure that the evaporative cooler you choose can cool 1 to 1.5 times the capacity of your greenhouse. The finest heat source is a professionally fitted and adequately vented heater, whether it is gas, oil, or wood-burning. Additionally, electric space heaters are beneficial. In most cases, patching the greenhouse into your home's heating system is insufficient, and installing a solar heating system is not cost-effective.

Cold-season crops such as peas, broccoli, beets, lettuce, and spinach require temperatures between fifty and seventy degrees Fahrenheit during the day and 45 to 55 degrees Fahrenheit at night. Beans, cucumbers, eggplants, peppers, and tomatoes are grown in the warm season prefer daytime temperatures of 60 to 85 degrees Fahrenheit and nocturnal temperatures of 55 to 65 degrees Fahrenheit. Herbs normally like temperatures between fifty-five and sixty degrees Fahrenheit at night and less than 85 degrees Fahrenheit during the day. Certain herbs, such as rosemary and basil, prefer slightly warmer nighttime temperatures of 65 to 70 degrees F.

Growing Medium

Gardeners with well-drained land can frequently construct their greenhouses without a floor, simply using the soil provided by nature. Fertilizers and amendments can be applied as needed; the tilled, amended soil can then be sterilized using a steam process that sustains a temperature of 180 degrees F for at least four hours. This process sterilizes the soil, eradicating any weed seeds, insects, or disease organisms present. If desired or changing the present soil is not practicable, elevated beds can also be constructed and filled with productive and rich soil. Unless you are a skilled gardener, resist the urge to produce greenhouse veggies hydroponically, as these methods are high-maintenance and punishing.

Pollination

Certain crops do not require insect pollination and can be produced without additional care in a greenhouse. However, some plants, such as cantaloupes, eggplants, tomatoes, and peppers, require pollination by bees or wind. Due to the absence of these two pollinators in the greenhouse, you may need to pollinate some of your greenhouse plants manually. Wind-pollinated plants can be gently shaken to release pollen from the male section of the plant and transport it to the female part. Other plants necessitate the removal of a male flower and rubbing it against a female blossom.

Additionally, a little paintbrush can be used to move pollen from one area of the plant to another. Male flowers have long, straight stems, but female blooms have a bulge of developing fruit beneath them. If you are experiencing difficulty pollination specific plant varieties, your local garden center should assist you.

Diseases and Pests

Due to the restricted environment and tight spaces, it is critical to immediately address any insect or disease concerns in the greenhouse. Avoid difficulties by following proper sanitation methods. Use only high-quality seed, disinfect instruments with a 5% bleach solution before transplanting seedlings, and prevent carrying dirt outdoors into the greenhouse on garden tools and shoes. Maintain a low humidity level and enough airflow throughout the greenhouse. After harvesting, remove spent plants and thoroughly clean the greenhouse's interior surfaces, as well as any instruments and equipment. If you see a problem, apply insecticides and fungicides immediately. Utilize only safe items to use on edible plants and always read and follow label guidelines.

3.3 The Best Food To Grow In A Greenhouse

Every summer, one of the most often grown crops in greenhouses is an overabundance of wonderfully good tomatoes. However, there is a large array of other easily grown edibles.

From out-of-season lettuces to large, mature aubergines, from tiny fiery chilies to hefty clusters of large, muscat golden grapes, a greenhouse may be a reliable source of not just homegrown food but also the finest, tastiest, and most sought-after luxury.

A greenhouse serves as a jumping-off place for vegetable production in the open. Along with fragile vegetables, while planning a greenhouse and the crops you'll grow inside, don't forget to include courgettes and outside cucumbers. You can use this method to jump-start runner beans, brassicas, and even root crops like carrots and beets.

Additionally, you can use a small amount of extra space to 'chit' seed potatoes, which means exposing them to light and warmth before planting to promote their shoots to begin growing. Your greenhouse can be used to grow a variety of fragile veggies. Your difficult choice will not be what to produce but what not to grow, as the room is always limited, and you will face some difficult choices.

GREENHOUSE GARDENING FOR BEGINNERS

Herbs

While many herbs are resilient and can be grown in the outdoor garden, several subtropical herbs thrive in a greenhouse's hotter, more humid weather.

Numerous others, such as rosemary, sage, and thyme, can also be grown in planters in a frost-free greenhouse during the winter to give a constant supply of aromatic leaves.

Basils, of which there are over 30 varieties available for sale in the UK, thrive in warm climates and have a variety of distinct flavors ranging from aniseed to citrus. They are used in a wide variety of recipes.

Additionally, the added warmth provided by a greenhouse will aid in synthesizing the fragrant oils that give basil its particular flavor. They are quite easy to grow from cuttings or seeds. Moreover, you can experiment and grow your galangal, ginger root, lemongrass, or cardamom. All of these are easily cultivated from root divisions obtained from specialty greengrocers.

Salad and Winter Greens

With a greenhouse, you'll be amazed and delighted at what may be grown out of season, something stores have helped us become accustomed to.

After the tomato crop, for example, you may plant Chinese greens like pak choi or others in greenhouse beds. Succulent leaves and stems can be expected by the end of October if seeds are put in cell trays in August and the crop is planted out in the early part of September.

Lettuce and rocket grow rapidly in fall and winter, but their growth will be less dense and more pulled up or 'leggy' than if planted in summer or spring. If there is no border soil, salad crops such as lettuce can be grown in large pots or growing bags.

Most seed firms also provide salad greens blends that are 'cut and come again.' These can be collected in small increments and will provide year-round greenery if planted at frequent intervals.

Fruit Production

Glasshouses were used to grow all kinds of off-season and exotic fruits in the days of the great Victorian estates, from peaches, figs, and apricots to bunches of luscious, big grapes and even pineapples.

Even if you lack the space for a large, stately glasshouse, a greenhouse is an excellent garden concept that will enable you to grow a variety of delectable fresh fruit harvests.

GREENHOUSE GARDENING FOR BEGINNERS

Citrus: While growing your lemons, kumquats, or calamondin oranges under glass is a possibility, the sweet-scented blossoms on these evergreen shrubs and trees are a sufficient reward. Lemon 'Verna', lemon/orange hybrid 'Meyer,' or calamondin orange can be grown in containers with the least winter temperature of 5 degrees.

Wall fruits: Fruit trees – typically fan-trained – will thrive in lean-to greenhouses if their high back wall gets adequate sun. If you have the wall space, the finest fruits to try are peaches, nectarines, apricots, and figs.

When the room is restricted, mini trees can be planted in huge pots to produce smaller crops. These miniature trees can be queued up or arranged outdoors during the summer.

Grapes: The freshness of grapes grown under glass in the United Kingdom exceeds that of grapes gathered outdoors. Extra care for your vine will repay you with magnificent grapes on enormous, well-shaped bunches. Preferably, the vine rootstock is grown outdoors, and the main stem is supplied into the greenhouse via the main stem.

This permits the roots to seek nutrients and water across a larger region while the remainder of the plant remains comfortably inside, benefiting from the warmer, longer growing season. However, vines cultivated entirely inside a greenhouse will flourish almost as well, and you can even harvest little crops from vines planted in huge pots.

3.4 Growing Without Soil

Growing plants in the absence of soil are not novel. The man began agriculture by cultivating plants in soil, but as an understanding of plant nutrition expanded, he discovered how to plant crops in artificial media such as sand, quartz, and gravel. The following step was to abandon solid media to grow plants in solutions directly. By 1860, the principles of plant growth in solution were well satisfactory and understood methods of providing nutrients to plants had been established. However, it was not until 1929 that the commercial potential of this approach was understood. The concept of growing plants in solution quickly gained popularity, with numerous pieces appearing in popular media. Numerous inflated and completely unfounded claims were made in support of this method of plant cultivation. This curiosity has persisted to the present day. This circular is meant to provide information on cultivating plants in the absence of soil.

Hydroponics

Hydroponics is the science, art, and practice of growing plants without soil, in which the vital elements for plant growth and development are supplied via a nutrient solution that gives all the nutrients the plants require in an accurate and consistent dose.

This approach received a significant boost during WWII when the American Armed Forces seized the technology to feed fresh greens and other crops aboard submarines and aircraft carriers, military outposts, volcanic islands, and polar regions and deserts. However, it is well established that the Babylonian Hanging Gardens and the Aztecs' floating gardens employed this gardening technique.

Hydroponics is best practiced in a greenhouse environment, where commercial and large-scale output is desired. However, the framework's simplicity necessary for a small crop makes it easy to establish hydroponic backyard gardens, terraces, or even in your kitchen.

Numerous hydroponic systems exist. They are distinguished by how the nutrient solution touches the roots.

GREENHOUSE GARDENING FOR BEGINNERS

New Growing System (NGS)

This recirculating hydroponic growth technique may be used with or without soil and is especially well-suited for growing strawberries and vegetables. This technology enables crops to grow in an ideal environment rich in water, oxygen, and nutrients. The NGS is a novel crop-growing system that utilizes flowing water and nutrients to produce high yields of great quality independent of the soil type.

The following are the advantages of the NGS over the conventional soil system:

1. A roughly 50% reduction in the use of fertilizers

2. Decreased water consumption by 70% to 95%

3. Reuse surplus water and nutrients, minimizing waste and expenses.

4. It enables a higher plant density per m2, resulting in a higher productivity per m2.

5. Is insensitive to local climatic circumstances

6. It is non-polluting because no fertilizers or pesticides are applied to the soil, and thus there is no risk of groundwater pollution.

Nutrient Film Technique System (NFT)

This approach includes growing plants in tubes that contain a solution of dissolved nutrients and water that is balanced to meet the needs of each plant type.

This system includes a reservoir for storing the nutrient solution. The nutrient solution is pumped from the reservoir to the top of the growth bench, where it passes through the channels and collects in the lower portion of the bed before being returned to the tank in a closed system.

Compared to conventional farming, this approach conserves between 80 and 90% of water.

Aeroponics

This approach involves stacking plants supported by root plugs and enabling the roots to directly absorb minute droplets or mists of the nutritional solution via sprinklers, resulting in optimal vegetal crop growth.

Aeroponics enables farmers and even homeowners to grow a great quantity of food in a little space. This model is distinguished by advanced technology, enabling farmers to earn a high-profit rate. The only disadvantage is the system's high deployment cost and the exact control of the entire process.

Semi-Hydroponic System

This approach is used to sustain flowers, fruit, and other crops with a highly developed root system. Channels, bags, or vases contain inert material such as perlite, peat, sand, stone wool, or coconut fiber. Percolation occurs as the nutrient solution percolates through this substance and is drained by the plant through a drip irrigation system. This system is commonly utilized in Europe, renowned for maximizing growing space utilization.

Aquaponics

Aquaponics is a symbiotic food production technology that combines hydroponics and conventional aquaculture.

Excreta from farmed animals can collect in water during ordinary aquaculture, increasing their toxicity. Nitrifying bacteria decompose by-products in the aquaponic system into nitrites and nitrates, which plants consume as nutrients in the hydroponic system. After that, the water is recirculated throughout the aquaculture system.

Since existing aquaculture and hydroponics techniques serve as the foundation for any aquaponic system, the amount, complexity, and type of food generated in an aquaponic system will vary depending on the method used.

This method of agriculture mixes fish farming and vegetable cultivation (Hydroponics) and has recently gained popularity among gardeners and environmentalists in the U.S and internationally. Especially in Australia, where droughts have increased interest in aquaponic cultivation, which uses up to 90% less water than traditional production methods.

Deep Floating Technique (DFT)

The name of this system comes from the absence of culture channels; instead, a cultivation table sits on a pool of nutrient solutions. Thus the term 'floating' hydroponics; unlike other forms of hydroponics, this one utilizes a sheet of nourishing fluid.

For the root system development of the seedlings and moisture retention and nutrient absorption, Spheroid plates are placed over the pool. The nutrient solution (about 4-5 cm deep) can seep up.

Because the roots of the plants are buried in the nutritional solution and thus stay throughout the cultivation time, extra attention must be paid to the solution's oxygenation.

Adsorbed-Nutrient Culture

Adsorption of plant nutrients on synthetic resins mimicking soil-clay particles is unique to this approach. These exchange elements are then combined with sand or gravel to provide the plant's nutritional requirements, just like colloids in natural soil do. This strategy has achieved great outcomes in the senior author's experimental work. Due to the high cost of the ion-exchange materials utilized, this technology is not commercially viable.

3.5 Selecting The Right Plants

Greenhouses have long been a necessary component of nursery operations and commercial producers. They enable these professionals to maintain a year-round supply of plants.

However, the advantages of greenhouses have increased their popularity among home growers. Apart from prolonging your growing season by allowing you to manage the temperature and humidity, a decent greenhouse has further benefits.

It enables you to exert control over a plant's environment and avoid disease transmission and attack by insects and pests. If you have a precious crop, a greenhouse can shelter it from four-legged pests such as rabbits and deer and bipedal pests such as thieves. Almost anything that can be grown outdoors can be grown indoors in a greenhouse, a cheaper greenhouse with fewer amenities.

Greenhouse Vegetables and Fruits

Simply because it is winter does not imply that you must accept the cardboard flavor of the majority of vegetables sold in ordinary supermarkets. Continue growing your fruits and vegetables in your greenhouse year-round for the best flavor, freshness, tenderness, and nutrition.

Warm-weather fruits and vegetables are ideal for greenhouse cultivation. Tomatoes, cucumbers, and winter or summer squash are all excellent possibilities. Eggplants are another excellent option.

Are you daydreaming about last summer's muskmelons and cantaloupes? Off-season, make your aspirations a reality by cultivating some in your greenhouse.

Not to be forgotten are peppers, which thrive in the sun and heat. You can produce anything from habanero peppers to bell peppers in your greenhouse, regardless of your taste preferences.

In French courts, persons of royal lineage used to maintain orangeries to cultivate oranges regardless of the weather. In your greenhouse, you can also produce citrus fruits. Citrus fruits such as lemons, oranges, and grapefruits are excellent selections.

If you reside in a cold environment, you can also enjoy fresh, nutritious greens and veggies during the winter. Kale, spinach, lettuce, and mustard greens will thrive in a greenhouse. Additionally, you can produce cool-weather crops such as peas, beets, carrots, and broccoli there.

Consider asparagus as a long-term complement. These plants can provide a continuous crop for up to 2 decades.

Greenhouse Ornamental Plants and Flowers

Nothing beats a bout of the winter blues like vibrant, lovely plants and flowers. Numerous types smell as gorgeous as they look, providing a true sensory delight.

Salvia, an ornamental sage, is an excellent choice for greenhouses. It is a species of the mint family and has a beautiful aroma. Salvia plants develop spikes of lovely, vibrant flowers.

During the off-season, you can grow a variety of other ornamentals and flowers in your greenhouse that you would plant outside in warmer weather. Geraniums, petunias and impatiens are just a few excellent choices.

GREENHOUSE GARDENING FOR BEGINNERS

If you adore the festive appearance of poinsettias, these are also excellent greenhouse plants. Consider storing some in your greenhouse to commemorate Christmas.

Ferns are finely shaped and colored, yet they can be difficult to grow. Consider raising some picky ferns in your greenhouse since you can manage the microclimate. They will reimburse you with beautiful green foliage and enthralling, exquisite displays.

Because your greenhouse can be as warm and humid as you wish, don't forget tropical plants. Orchids, for example, are a possibility. Another example is fascinating carnivorous plants such as Venus flytraps. Reduce the humidity yet maintain a high temperature in your greenhouse to cultivate thorny cacti.

Greenhouse Herbs

With all the fresh produce you'll be growing, you'll want to stock up on herbs and spices. Reduce your reliance on high-priced groceries by producing your own. You'll also enhance the flavor of your dishes and provide more nutrients for you and your family when you use fresh herbs.

Anything capable of growing outdoors will thrive in a greenhouse. Mint, rosemary, and sage are all good choices, as are parsley, thyme, and cilantro.

3.6 Planting In A Warm And Cold Weather

Growing anything in an unheated greenhouse during the chilly winter months may seem impossible. Unfortunately, it is not! The keys to success are understanding how to operate an unheated greenhouse and which plants are most suited.

Greenhouse in winter

As the nights grow shorter and the days become cooler, you may question if you can still utilize your greenhouse. Yes, indeed! Numerous plants may be grown in a greenhouse during the cold, and while they may not grow as quickly as they would during the summertime, they will still thrive with some shelter from the outdoors.

The precise crops you should plant will vary depending on the sort of greenhouse you have and your location, but there are a few crops that work well for all, as long as you plan!

How To Clean A Greenhouse For Winter

Before growing for the winter season, give your greenhouse a thorough cleaning. While this is not the most pleasant of tasks, it is critical. Eliminating tenacious dirt, mold and algae allow for more light to enter, which benefits your winter plants - after all, they require all the light they can get! Additionally, this is an excellent time to do it because you will have fewer tasks to complete in the rest of the garden.

If possible, choose a mild and dry day for the task.

Then take the following steps:

- Clear all plants from the greenhouse and relocate them to a safe location while you work your magic.
- Sweep or vacuum the interior to remove any debris.
- Using a disinfectant, clean all structural components of the greenhouse. This might be a solution tailored to the garden or a general household cleaning. The hottest solutions are the most effective!
- Scrub and soak each panel of glass with a glass cleaner.

Growing Herbs In A Greenhouse In Winter

Fresh herbs make all the difference in cooked food, and there is no reason to forego them simply because the weather changes. While certain herbs will not thrive in the UK's harsh winter climate, others will bloom when planted under glass.

Coriander, mint and dill are all excellent alternatives for late autumn planting. Parsley, for example, is a good cold-weather herb; it grows to a respectable size and can even sprout through a little dusting of snow! Although Mediterranean herbs such as thyme and sage despise winter and moisture, they may survive in a greenhouse climate. Take cuttings and put them tightly together in some dry soil in the summer. When May arrives, you can transplant them outside into a herb garden.

Vegetables To Grow In A Greenhouse In Winter

Numerous hardy veggies will thrive indoors throughout the winter - here are our top recommendations:

Winter Lettuce

Salad lovers will like the fact that several varieties of lettuce prefer a milder climate. A little gem, rocket, and lamb's lettuce are all excellent choices - they grow quickly, so harvest when you have some large leaves to use.

Potatoes

Potatoes are the ideal winter ingredient and can be grown in grow sacks, a large flower pot, or a bucket. Fill your container two-thirds with garden soil and one-third with compost for optimal results. Potatoes grown early in the winter will be ready to harvest in March; alternatively, you can plant them later and then transplant them outside as the weather warms. Potatoes are frost-sensitive, so maintain a warm greenhouse if the weather drops drastically.

Pak choi

This oriental vegetable pairs beautifully with stir-fries and noodle dishes. Vitamin-rich and quick to develop can be planted as late as October for winter harvesting. Leaves take approximately 30 days to mature, whereas the entire plant takes 70 days.

Broccoli and cabbage

If you maintain an optimal temperature in your greenhouse, broccoli and cabbage can thrive throughout the winter. Plant them early (mid-winter) to be ready to go outside in the spring.

Kale And Spinach

These hardy leafy greens thrive in the cold, making them ideal for growing over the winter. While growth times may vary, you're certain to have an abundance of crops. Spinach types such as Riccio d'Asti and Merlo Nero are suitable for sowing in an unheated greenhouse, while kale can tolerate temperatures as low as -6C.

Brussel sprouts

Whether you despise or adore them, brussels sprouts are ideal for winter greenhouses. They take approximately three months to mature, so pick them up in March when they reach a diameter of approximately 1-2 inches. If you're planning to cook them, harvest sprouts that are similar in size - this will provide a more consistent cooking time.

Insulating A Greenhouse For Winter

Greenhouses are an excellent method to keep your enthusiasm for gardening alive during the colder months, but they must retain their heat adequately, especially when the temperatures begin to drop. It is critical to have adequate insulation; we propose utilizing horticultural plastic bubble wrap to shield your plants from Ultraviolet radiation while keeping costs down. We recommend insulating only the top and end glass to eliminate any damp issues. In this manner, you'll maintain convenient access to your plants while maintaining appropriate light levels.

GREENHOUSE GARDENING FOR BEGINNERS

To maintain your greenhouse over freezing, you'll almost certainly need to add some more heat. The ideal heating system is electric, and when controlled by a thermostat, it does not have to be prohibitively expensive. If your greenhouse lacks electricity, a paraffin heater is an excellent substitute.

Winter Greenhouse Ventilation

While insulation is critical, so is airflow – and striking the right mix is critical. Along with the heat, your plants require a sufficient amount of co2 to prevent becoming leggy, as well as sufficient oxygen for nighttime transpiration. Humidity also inhibits plant growth, so proper winter greenhouse airflow is critical to avoid disease or fungal buildup.

Open the greenhouse doors in the early morning light and shut them before sunset.

When it comes to growing plants in a greenhouse throughout the winter, your possibilities may be greater than you believe! The best course of action is to give it a try; experiment with different types of plants in various pots and enjoy the tasty fruits!

Greenhouse in Summers

Year-round vegetable cultivation in a greenhouse enables you to enjoy fresh fruit and vegetables at any time. Even the most heat-tolerant plants may struggle in the greenhouse's heat during the summer months. To maintain correct temperatures inside your greenhouse, consider climate control solutions such as shade cloths, ventilation, and evaporative cooling.

Monitoring Greenhouse Temperature

Make sure you have a thermometer in the greenhouse so you can keep tabs on the temperature there all day long. The majority of plants flourish in temperatures between 70 and 80 degrees Fahrenheit during the day.

While some veggies may survive increased temperatures, severe heat should be avoided. Tomatoes yield less fruit when the temperature exceeds 95 degrees, whereas peppers shed blooms and generate sterile pollen when the temperature exceeds 90 degrees.

As the temperature rises, water the veggies more regularly to prevent wilting. Maintain wet soil but avoid oversaturating it and drowning your vegetables. If your greenhouse is equipped with an automatic watering system, inspect it periodically for leaks and clogged filters during the summer months.

Cooling Your Greenhouse

Fans and ventilation provide sufficient airflow in many climates to prevent your greenhouse from scorching during the summer months. Vents should be installed on the walls or the roof of every greenhouse. Ascertain that they are open and, if possible, remove part of the roof and side panels to allow heat to exit the greenhouse and improve ventilation. Installing vents can chill your greenhouse by up to ten degrees, depending on the ambient temperature and wind conditions.

Adding fans can improve temperature control and airflow even more. Employ exhaust fans that draw warm air out of the greenhouse to allow fresh air and cooling entry. While air conditioning is too expensive for greenhouses, the cooling effect can reduce temperatures by 20 degrees more than vents alone.

Tinting the greenhouse from direct sunlight is another efficient approach to keep temperatures in check. If you are creating a greenhouse for the first time in a hot environment, try placing it in the shade of trees. If this is not possible, consider placing shade cloths on the greenhouse's exterior. To keep the plants safe from direct sunshine, you can hang shade curtains within the greenhouse.

Greenhouse Planting Guide

Even if you grow veggies year-round in a greenhouse, you will want to sow seeds appropriately. Attempting to plant cool-season crops such as lettuce, cauliflower, and beets during the summer may result in the vegetables being damaged or seed germination being prevented. For example, lettuce will not sprout if the soil temperature exceeds 80 to 85 degrees. Greens may also generate flower stalks to reproduce and may become unpleasant if the temperature rises too high.

Rotate your crops to produce cool-season veggies, and hot-weather vegetables flourish when the hot summer heat arrives. Consider peppers, tomatoes, maize, zucchini, beans, and summer squash as heat-tolerant summer greenhouse crops.

Even warm-season veggies can be harmed by excessive heat. Tomatoes, for example, may suffer from flower abortion and sterile pollen, as well as irregular fruit, ripening and sunscald harm.

Shading a Greenhouse

Shade paints are an easy and cost-effective approach to reduce the sun's intensity. You can add additional layers as the summer progresses and then rinse and brush them off as the temperature drops. Shade paint may not be appropriate for all greenhouses, particularly those with unpainted wood, in which case blinds and netting come in handy.

Internal or external blinds are available. Exterior blinds are the most successful since they screen the sunlight before entering the room through the glass. They can be removed on cooler days. They may, however, obstruct efficient vent functioning, so you'll need to find a workaround. Alternatively, spend a little more and install inside blinds, which can also be motorized. Mesh or shade netting is a less expensive alternative to blinds easily held in place with clips.

Ventilating a Greenhouse

One of the most effective ways to counter heat is by giving plants adequate airflow. Ventilation provided by roof vents, side vents (typically louvered), and the greenhouse door can provide the necessary air circulation to cool hot plants.

Every two minutes, an area of roof ventilation equal to one-fifth of the floor area provides a full air exchange. In most greenhouses, this percentage of roof outlets is a luxury, but opening doors and side vents can circulate the air sufficiently.

Temperatures greater than roughly 27°C (81°F) can start to harm some plants, so keep a minimum-maximum thermometer on standby to keep an eye on things. On bright days, venture out as early as possible to open all vents and doors and leave them open throughout the night. You can keep out local wildlife and cats by placing netting over the door, but make sure the netting enables pollinators to get through.

Automatic vent openers can be installed to automate the procedure partially, but because they typically respond slowly, you'll still need to be present to open the door and begin the cooling process.

3.7 Scheduling plants for the year-round growing

Scheduling is critical in the production of greenhouse crops. Schedules must be precise to grow crops to marketable size at the appropriate time of year. Due to poor timing, growers may encounter undersized or non-flowering plants, overgrown plants during the peak of the season, or empty benches with many weeks of selling season remaining. Numerous factors can affect the completion timing of bedding plants, such as the maturity of liners and plugs, their growing conditions, the average daytime temperature, photoperiod, the usage of plant growth regulators, and the size of the finish container. Calendar age, i-e, Chronological age vs. physiological age of the plant, is a constant source of contention, and production decisions impact crop timing.

To schedule a crop successfully, the grower must first establish the week of the year during which the crop will be marketed and then work backward to calculate the seed sowing or planting date. If seedlings, liners or plugs are purchased, shipping and transplantation dates must be established.

Let's begin by emphasizing the critical nature of day length, which is likely the most critical component in deciding your greenhouse planting timetable. If you are not utilizing additional lighting, you must be aware of the usual day lengths for your area at various times of the year. In early February, where we live in Colorado, our day duration begins to exceed 10 hours each day, which is normally sufficient daylight for seeds to grow. And by mid-November, our days will have decreased to less than ten hours, and plant development will have slowed dramatically. Plants will survive the winter but will often enter a state of semi-hibernation. If you start your winter garden early, the plants will reach maturity by late November, and you will be able to pick from the semi-dormant plants throughout the winter, even without supplementary lighting.

GREENHOUSE GARDENING FOR BEGINNERS

The other factor to consider when planning your greenhouse growing schedule is the climate inside the greenhouse and the several microclimates that may exist. Typically, the coldest areas in your greenhouse will be near your greenhouse windows and directly adjacent to your vents. That is where you should store your cold-hardy veggies, such as spinach and kale, throughout the winter. Typically, the warmest portion of your greenhouse will be along the north wall, where the sun shines off and strikes the plants. By timing your greenhouse growing schedule around the length of the day, regulating your plants' position depending on temperature, and selecting the appropriate crops and kinds, you may produce veggies year-round.

February:

Begin sowing your first round of cold-tolerant crops in the spring (lettuce, radishes, kale, beets, peas, carrots, etc.).

In the greenhouse, begin planting long-season, warm-loving vegetable crops (peppers, tomatoes, eggplant, etc.). These crops normally mature in 100-150 days and do not handle winter temperatures, so plan to keep them in a warm growing area for as long as possible while they mature and ripen their fruit. These crops can be started indoors and transplanted outside once overnight temperatures reliably exceed 55 degrees. Alternatively, you can keep them blooming in your greenhouse throughout the summer and into the fall.

March/April:

During the spring equinox, the days get longer, and the greenhouse plants begin to grow faster. Begin seeding warm-season crops that require fewer days to mature (cucumbers, basil, beans, squash).

Harvest the first batch of cold-tolerant plants and keep planting cold-tolerant, fast-growing crops in their place.

May:

The longer days and hotter nights enable your greenhouse to expand at a much faster rate.

You'll almost certainly be gathering a lot of spinach, kale, lettuce, and peas.

If you began transplants in the greenhouse, you could now begin planting cold-tolerant transplants (cauliflower, broccoli, cabbage) outside once nighttime temperatures consistently exceed 45 degrees and hot transplants outside once nighttime temperatures consistently exceed 55 degrees (tomatoes, peppers, eggplant).

GREENHOUSE GARDENING FOR BEGINNERS

June/July:

This is a particularly hot time of year for greenhouses, based on the cooling system used. Your warm crops, such as eggplant, peppers, beans, and tomatoes, will thrive in the greenhouse, but you must monitor for overheating and ensure adequate ventilation and humidity to prevent the plants from transpiring excessively and wilting.

August/September:

This is typically the best time to begin planting your winter garden. From November to January, the day length shortens to the point when plants grow very slowly without additional lighting. With a winter garden, the idea is to sow early enough that most plants are close to fruition by November or December. As plant production decreases, your crops will enter a semi-hibernation state, allowing you to harvest gradually throughout the winter, even if there is little new growth visible.

Before the first frost in your location, it's also a good opportunity to bring some potted plants within for the winter. Outside, peppers, figs, citrus, and tomatoes can survive the winter in planters in the greenhouse.

GREENHOUSE GARDENING FOR BEGINNERS

October:

The days are becoming shorter. You've already planted your winter garden, but October still provides enough light to start crops with a short growing cycle (such as radishes, which mature in 20-30 days) or to start crops for harvest in late winter/early spring, realizing they will mature very slowly during the winter.

Hardy crops such as lettuce, spinach, and kale sowed now have a good chance of germinating and developing into little plants, overwintering, and growing fast as the days extend in February. Winter and early spring veggies have a richer flavor than other times of the year because vegetables begin storing sugars in their cell walls to stave off frost damage.

November/December/January:

A period of dormancy and rest preceding the start of the new season. Harvest cautiously from mature plants, removing kale leaves, excavating beets and carrots, or cutting spinach. This is also the time to prune your fruit trees for the winter, examine seed catalogs, and plan next year's garden.

If supplementary lighting is used, greenhouse development does not need to be slowed during this time. Leafy greens and root crops will flourish in your winter greenhouse with a little additional light. Winter greenhouses have also been used to grow warm-weather crops such as tomatoes and peppers with extra illumination if the greenhouse's nightly temperatures remain above 62 degrees. Because a Ceres greenhouse captures light by reflecting its north, east, and west walls, we may need less additional lighting during the winter to maintain excellent growth.

Here is a general greenhouse planting chart:

Month	Plants
February	Kale, Lettuce, Radishes, Carrots, Beets, Peas, Peppers, Tomatoes, Eggplant, Etc
March/April	Squash, Basil, Beans, Cucumbers
May	Lettuce, Spinach, Kale, Peas, Cauliflower, Cabbage, Peppers, Broccoli, Tomatoes, Eggplant
June July	Peppers, Beans, Eggplant, And Tomatoes
August September	Citrus, Peppers, Figs And Tomatoes
October	Radishes, Lettuce, Spinach, And Kale
November December January	Root Vegetables Like Carrots, Kale, And Beets And Leafy Greens

Chapter 4
Maintaining The Greenhouse

The plants will not thrive if left to their own devices. You must maintain your greenhouse to ensure that your plants reach their maximum potential.

The following are some methods for greenhouse maintenance:

4.1 Maintenance

Ventilation and Heating

Proper ventilation is critical. Heat is deadly to plants. Conduct routine inspections and maintenance on all heating parts of the system, particularly before the winter.

Consider adding a second door to prevent heat loss due to a draught. This creates additional passageways for warm air to escape.

GREENHOUSE GARDENING FOR BEGINNERS

Colors can also have a role in temperature management. Darker hues absorb more heat than lighter colors. Indoor surfaces should be painted black to retain and attract heat.

It is a good idea to install roof vents along the ridgeline of the greenhouse's ceiling and roof. Or temperature control systems that are widely available for purchase. Additionally, you might install ventilation fans to assist with air movement.

Sun and shade

Plants require sunlight to survive. We are powerless to prevent dust from accumulating on top of your greenhouse coverings. Thus, a simple wiping will suffice. Clean the windows of your greenhouse regularly to allow for more sunlight. We are not interested in seeing a dusty greenhouse now, are we?

Alternatively, some natural shadow will suffice. Deciduous trees should be planted surrounding your greenhouse to provide shadow during the summer and sun during the winter. Additionally, it is ideal for sheltering against high winds.

If there is insufficient space outside for cultivating trees, you can install artificial shades. Install roll-up blinds within the greenhouse to shield plants from the summer sun when necessary.

Maintaining humidity

It's all about humidity. The greenhouse's humidity level should be as high as possible. Plants require humidity to grow.

Regularly water your plants. Never overwater your plants. Excessive amounts are dangerous, as they can completely drown out your plants.

Consider the method of dampening. Additionally, it aids in maintaining proper humidity levels for your plants. Moistening the hard surfaces in your greenhouse causes the wet surfaces to evaporate, increasing humidity.

Take care when using anti-dripping linings. If you see water drips, it's time to relocate the plants in the drip line.

Monitoring pests

When choosing the best greenhouse care, which is a critical component of pest management, prevention is always preferable to treatment. To avoid pests, avoid bringing them within your greenhouse.

Inspect new plants thoroughly before bringing them inside your greenhouse. If you are already experiencing pest problems, conduct a study about your circumstance. For example, if you discover aphids on your plants, you will understand how beneficial ladybugs are.

Natural enemies exist for pests that wreak havoc on your plants. This group of insects includes lady beetles, lacewings, parasite flies, and adult assassin bugs. You can include them in the greenhouse to aid in pest management.

Cleanliness and orderliness

When it comes to growth, hygiene is critical. Keeping the environment clean is an extremely efficient method of preventing pests: wash benches and tables with soapy water to eliminate grime.

Scrub and mop your smooth floors regularly if you have them. It's pleasant to walk through a clean, well-organized greenhouse. Ensure that you wipe the windows. Wipe down all surfaces. Additionally, sweep floors to remove fallen leaves.

Plant care

Plant cultivation is one of the most significant functions of the greenhouse. As a result, taking care of the garden should be a priority. Why would you construct a greenhouse devoid of plants?

There are some fundamentals to plant care. Dead branches and leaves should be pruned and removed from the greenhouse. Dead stems and leaves may suck out nutrients intended for other plant sections. As a result, deleting them is the wisest course of action.

Eliminate weeds and other invasive species from the area surrounding the greenhouse. Weeds deplete the nutrients available to your plants. Eliminating them should allow your plants to flourish.

Repairs

With time, certain components of your greenhouse will deteriorate in strength. They are constantly checking to see if the materials are still stable.

Examine everything that requires repair. As though your covers were torn. Restore damaged vents. Repaint shaded areas if the paint has worn off.

4.2 High Tunnels, Low Tunnels, Coldframes, Hoop Houses, and Polytunnels

They are known as "cold frames" because of their ability to serve as overwintering structures. These simple hoop structures are utilized by nursery producers all over the world for dormant crops that don't require heat. They sounded like a Cold Frame since they didn't have heat. There is less environmental control in nurseries' cold frames compared to those found in greenhouses.

A single-piece Quonset or two-piece Gothic arch can be used for cold frame construction; the latter is taller but easier to move. Poles composed of normal agricultural dirt pounded into the ground connect arches to purlins. It is possible for nursery stock to be left or relocated as requested by the farmer by removing the white overwintering plastic in the springtime.

Quonset huts are known as "hoop homes" because of the Quonset arch that sits on top of a cold frame. Although the Hoop House's name was changed to reflect its ability to grow crops year-round, the structure's essential design remains the same. Greenhouse-grade poly is used for cold frames by Hoop House farmers instead of white overwintering cover. Hundreds of farms have turned to cold frames as an affordable first greenhouse because of their ability to provide natural ventilation or fan ventilation through roll-up sides. An appropriate habitat for the growth of many different plants can be provided by a series of Cold frames with their limited air volume and unique climate.

Cold frames with white overwintering poly can be deemed Polytunnels if they have a second layer of four-year greenhouse plastic on top. In many parts of the world, Polytunnel is a better name for these Cold Frame Hoop Houses.

High Tunnel was coined to separate commercial Coldframe construction from low-framed box known as a "Cold Frame" by gardeners. Low-tech greenhouses like cold frames have gained popularity in recent years. It became known as the "High Tunnel" because workers were able to walk under the hoops of the Coldframes because they were only 7-10 feet high.

With anchor posts shoved into the ground rather than supported by a solid concrete foundation, High Tunnels are considered temporary constructions. Heating high tunnels in the winter are possible using unit heaters, although they are more usually utilized as unheated buildings to extend the growing cycle of crops typically uncovered throughout the summer.

Side-connected In some manufacturers' definitions of High Tunnels, hoop houses (also known as Crop Protector at GGS) are included, while others restrict the word to single arch structures, such as Cold frames. You must know exactly what you want from a High Tunnel before acquiring one.

Low Tunnels are an excellent option for growers who don't want to raise their hoop height. Lower, narrower hoops, especially for ground cover, are preferred by many growers. Low tunnels are the obvious choice for these gardeners.

GREENHOUSE GARDENING FOR BEGINNERS

Scan the follow QR Code
to receive your FREE bonus

Chapter 5
Making a profit

Not only are greenhouses a fixture of botanical gardens. Additionally, they provide a year-round source of veggies. Those vegetables have the potential to provide revenue for you and your family. By growing veggies that are not generally available during the winter or are inaccessible in a specific area, you can earn profit by offering your greenhouse veggies at farmer's markets or directly to clients.

5.1 Why Greenhouse Business?

Having a Greenhouse is akin to owning a company. You would be unaware that you have already subconsciously aided nature in addition to generating wealth. It is a green enterprise that may also assist you with your wants and consumptions.

For individuals who already have a greenhouse and enjoy it as a pastime. To that end, this section may be of great assistance in enlightening you that apart from pastime. Additionally, you can use it as a source of revenue.

Maintaining a greenhouse can also be a source of relaxation for humans. The bright and fresh-looking leaves are pleasing and restful to human sight. Additionally, it creates healthy oxygen and meals.

Therefore, you must care for it and perhaps love it completely. Not only for financial gain and personal fulfillment but also the benefit of the natural surroundings.

5.2 Make Money Growing Vegetables in Greenhouses

1. Take into account your business concept. If you must transport veggies from your greenhouse to farmers' markets or other outlets, consider the distance and transportation expense. These expenses take a bite out of your overall revenue. Recognize that location is crucial if you choose to have people come to you. Ascertain that your greenhouse is located near a large market or densely inhabited area.
2. Ensure the product's quality. Consistently producing high-quality products is critical to the profitability of your greenhouse. People will not travel great distances

to buy your products or visit your greenhouse if they can obtain the same vegetable quality in a grocery store. Even if it costs more, invest in the best seeds and technologies available to ensure that your consumers return.

3. Conduct research and make informed decisions about the crops you will cultivate in your greenhouse. Grow vegetables that are not accessible in your area at specific periods of the year to maximize profits. Greenhouse gardeners can harvest at any time of year, which is a huge advantage for providing fresh veggies in areas not in season.

4. Maintain an eye on your greenhouse's expenses. Following your initial crop, you may be overjoyed with the additional revenue. However, analyze how much of that revenue was spent on growing the produce, selling the crop, and greenhouse maintenance. Keep a close eye on the money you earn, and it is required to earn it. Understanding the distinction is critical to success.

5.3 Growing Flowers in a Greenhouse for Profit

A greenhouse may enable you to convert your flower planting hobby into a profitable side job or perhaps a year-round business. And while constructing a greenhouse or laying water and electrical connections requires a significant initial cost, if done correctly, you must be able to recoup your investment fairly quickly.

Identifying a Market for Flower Sales

Before you construct a greenhouse in your garden, you must locate a market for the flowers you raise. Clients will not materialize out of anywhere - if there is no one in your neighborhood willing to buy flowers, do not begin your greenhouse business.

Geographical location

To begin, determine the geographical area in which you will sell flowers. Selling locally is generally where most people will begin, and it's an excellent place to start because conducting market research on a local scale is extremely simple. Additionally, selling flowers locally costs less than shipping them to another state or city.

Once established, do not limit yourself to selling flowers locally. If you have the funds, keep in mind that you can grow your firm throughout the state or perhaps nationally. Nowadays, this is particularly easy, as developing a website or app is not particularly difficult.

Type of flowers

It may appear as though selecting a flower to cultivate is a matter of personal preference. This is correct; however, selecting flowers is also a component of selecting a market.

You should select a flower category that is currently in demand. While you may adore orchids, you should plant something different if there is no market for them in your region. Consider the kind of flowers that are popular in your area and choose easily grown ones.

If you're not sure where to begin, some of the most popular and easy-to-grow greenhouse flowers include the following:

- Amazon lilies.
- Chrysanthemums.
- Orchids.
- Petunias.
- Chinese hibiscus.
- Roses.
- African violets.

Additionally, you should likely pick one to three flowers that you are quite adept at growing rather than ten flowers with which you are unfamiliar. You can allocate your efforts more efficiently and develop strong relationships with fewer clients by narrowing your expertise early on.

Furthermore, it will be difficult for a newly created business to focus on everything, so it's a good reason to begin small and expand as needed.

Additionally, understand that different flowers require varying amounts of light, humidity, temperature, and water. It's considerably simpler to cultivate and care for a small number of flowers with identical requirements.

Type of customer

Then you must decide who will purchase your flowers:

- You may directly sell flowers to customers.
- You may offer flowers to bulk clients, such as florists.

Whether you choose to cater to one type of client or both, you'll need to approach each one differently. While sales to bulk clients can account for most of your profit, you will need to secure a continuous production of flowers, possibly throughout the year.

Additionally, you'll need to focus on your wholesale cost, often 35% to 50% less than retail pricing. It's difficult to provide accurate figures for flower pricing because markets vary widely. However, it would help if you generally chose a pricing plan to satisfy both you and your buyer.

Marketing Your Business

You must develop a website and utilize local SEO, given the likelihood of selling locally. If you are unfamiliar with this term, make sure to conduct extra research. Nowadays, people first do when they need anything is Google it.

Following that, utilize Google's My Business tool. It will once again assist you in reaching out to potential clients searching for flowers online.

Do not overlook classic marketing strategies such as direct mail newsletters, posters, and so forth. These are often more expensive, but they reach those who cannot be reached digitally.

5.4 Your Responsibilities

Finally, keep in mind that you'll have a few responsibilities as a greenhouse business owner.

Your first obligation is to look after your flowers. A greenhouse will preserve your plants from ever-changing exterior circumstances, but it is up to you to assure that everything in your greenhouse is just right, from temperature to light.

Then, depending on the number of items you sell, who you sell to, and local tax requirements, you may be required to obtain a tax identification number. Regardless of your location, you will normally be required to collect sales tax from customers or record that you sell flowers wholesale. Consult your local laws to determine what to do.

Finally, keep in mind that you must treat it as a business if you wish to benefit from your greenhouse pastime. Flower sales will not become your principal source of income overnight. You must be dedicated to your task and consistent in your performance. Additionally, if you lack time to devote to flower growth, you can employ someone to do it for you.

Conclusion

The primary purpose of a greenhouse garden is to lengthen the growing season of treasured crops and plants. Horticulture enthusiasts should also be enthused about greenhouses since they allow for the year-round cultivation of plants and flowers that can subsequently be taken into the house. A greenhouse garden can be constructed inexpensively or extravagantly, using plastic or glass, and can be appealing or just utilitarian in appearance. After selecting an ideal place for your greenhouse garden, you can construct one yourself by obtaining a greenhouse kit from one of several renowned manufacturers. These are do-it-yourself projects that can be as intricate or as simple as desired, huge or small.

The recommendations in this guide will help you get started on your blossoming greenhouse gardening experience and ensure that your greenhouse investment is worthwhile in terms of time, money, and effort. With a greenhouse, any season becomes planting season. Take pleasure in the joy of serving homegrown fruits and vegetables at your dinner table. Have fun gardening throughout the year!

Without the necessary equipment, a greenhouse is useless. This ebook contains all the necessary information about the equipment and where to put your plants. Check appropriate plant temperatures and make the most of your garden space by extending the seasons. This entails cultivating veggies in the winter and then using your greenhouse to begin seedlings as the weather warms up. When the weather is truly warm, tomatoes and other heat-loving crops can be transplanted. Maintain a laser-like focus to achieve tangible outcomes.

Hence, this book is an excellent resource for beginners interested in starting their greenhouse, whether for commercial interests or simply as a hobby!